Small Corner of the Stars

poems by

Paul Stroble

Finishing Line Press
Georgetown, Kentucky

Small Corner of the Stars

For Beth and Emily

Copyright © 2017 by Paul Stroble
ISBN 978-1-63534-348-9 First Edition
All rights reserved under International and Pan-American Copyright Conventions. No part of this book may be reproduced in any manner whatsoever without written permission from the publisher, except in the case of brief quotations embodied in critical articles and reviews.

ACKNOWLEDGMENTS

"Carnegie Library" (as "Billy"), "Lucy's Salon," "Haircut at Elmer's" (as "At Elmer's") appeared in *Springhouse*.
"Questions" appeared in *Pegasus*.
"Garage Science": "Bombastium" is a fictional chemical element in the Donald Duck comics.
"Bagworms in the Hands of an Angry Homeowner" incorporates a few phrases from the famous Jonathan Edwards sermon.
"Psalm in Snow" incorporates images from Psalm 23, Psalm 19:3-4, Psalm 147:16, Job 38:22, 25, 31, Matthew 6:29-30. The poem is dedicated to the amazing women pastors whom I've known over the years.

Many thanks to the St. Louis Poetry Center, Dwight Bitikofer, Mary Biddinger, Heather Derr-Smith, Jane Ellen Ibur, Stacey Stachowicz, Susan Croce Kelly, the Novel Neighbor Bookstore, the Webster Groves Starbucks, and especially my friend and mentor Tom Dukes, who helped me realize my poetry dreams. These childhood experiences are fictionalized, but I remember my late parents, Paul and Mildred Stroble; my excellent hometown teachers of science and literature, including the late Don Snyder and the late Jim Coleman; and also another dear friend, Jim's wife Peggy Coleman. Many thanks to Leah Maines and everyone at FLP.

Publisher: Leah Maines
Editor: Christen Kincaid
Cover Art: Henri-Edmond Cross, Landscape with Stars (c. 1905-1908),
    Metropolitan Museum of Art.
Author Photo: Beth Stroble
Cover Design: Elizabeth Maines McCleavy

Printed in the USA on acid-free paper.
Order online: www.finishinglinepress.com
    also available on amazon.com

Author inquiries and mail orders:
Finishing Line Press
P. O. Box 1626
Georgetown, Kentucky 40324
U. S. A.

Table of Contents

Questions 1
Asbury Tree 3
Sick Kid 4
Vicky 5
Summer Sky 6
Carnegie Library 7
Miss Audie's Scotland Slides 8
Last Meeting of the Williams Pond Goose Hunting Club 9
Summer 11
Lucy's Salon 13
1962 14
Cemetery Caretaker 15
Garage Science 16
Bagworms in the Hands of an Angry Homeowner 17
Friends on the Nickel Plate Tracks 18
Summer Band 19
Dair-E-Hut 20
Robot King of Mars 21
Indermark Crossing 22
Family Trip 23
Happiness 25
Kryptonite on July 4th 26
Haircut at Elmer's 27
Morels 28
Country Pastor 29
First Advent Sunday 30
Small-Town December Saturday 31
Paved with Stars 33
Psalm in Snow 34

Questions

It's a sleepy class in philosophy,
at noon, and everyone is hungry, too,
so, heads up, I toss a question.
Does God make everything happen?

        Yes, because he's God.

But what about the bad things?

        No, not the bad things.

        I believe everything has a purpose.

That doesn't mean he causes everything.

*Just because he knows what will happen doesn't mean
he causes things to happen.*

        Then why does he allow things to happen?

*Maybe it's for our education,
        or for some mysterious purpose.
      If a child dies, for instance, God must have a reason.*

        My God wouldn't let a child die intentionally.

What do you mean, your God?

God calls us to him when it's our time.

        *But I don't want to sit next to the guy on the plane
        whose time has come.*

Weeks later, at 31,000 feet, people sit in various states
of repose. The woman across the aisle sleeps snoring.
The man behind her reads a magazine. My wife
plays Go Fish with our young daughter. Home for Christmas.

Here come the attendants with drinks.
But the pilot announces turbulence over Kansas City.
It seems not the time to toss the question again.

Asbury Tree

White oak by the white church,
a branch blesses the roof.
The trunk is large enough
to go to church in a strong wind.

Cut it at your peril, pastor or lay,

for Miss Audie gave her heart to the Lord
beneath that tree when she was seven,
seventy years ago and three.

May it stand seven times seventy
and become earth's living thing, guardian
of country churches in succession,
a place thin for Spirit,
shade for pressed hands.

Sick Kid

101 degrees.
He used a box of tissues in a day.
His Dick Tracy character's name is Mucus.

Green toy soldiers on the blanket
substitute for police and criminals.
Flattop got pushed into the throw-up bucket
and Mom, spreading tender care, washed him
before Tracy dragged him off to jail.

Dad brings library books.
Midday, he sleeps.
But good cartoons come on TV
at 3, and the Three Stooges at 4:30:
crowbar-up-the-nose fun
with his toast with butter, cinnamon sugar,
lime soda in a glass.

Kids play outside next door
as he stays in bed, losing weight.
Young, he's still philosophical.
We're born in bed. Grandpa
died in bed. A third of our lives are in bed.

Bed.... the womb of the covers,
mountain range on a distant world,
a rugged terrain for crime fighting,
the secret place for prayers, sorrow,
hopes for world peace, wellness.

Vicky

Good god, what is that? I thought when I saw
your eyelash curler on the floor beside the toilet.

I studied your apartment,
all the girl stuff I never saw before

because I've no sisters, and I was young then.
I saw the box of tampons, which I did know about,

and the hairbrush full of your wavy hair,
and flowery soaps. You were a slob,

but I liked that about you,
and from your bedroom window

I could see our park where we played as neighbor kids,
the hills we ran, the swing set,

the merry-go-round where you sent me round and round
until I was so dizzy.

Summer Sky

Dogs fuss in the humid
midsummer, half-quarter
moon above Rachel Park,
fireflies flicker by the swing set,
the willow trees bow,
still grieving last November.

On my bedroom wall,
a Rand McNally map
of the solar system,
what we knew then: twelve moons
for Jupiter, nine for Saturn,
Uranus five, Neptune two, and Pluto.

Find the Big Dipper, said Dad,
and you can find the North Star,
and now you can draw with
your eyes the Little Dipper.
Find the brightest star, then
you can draw Canis Major...

Bobby and I studied.
Hey, that's Orion. No, it's not.
Yes, it is. You're an asshole.
Junior scientists, field work
advancing human knowledge.

We just mapped our own.
There is Soda Bottle, pouring
stars into the night. There
is our creek, there is an apple,
and there is President Kennedy.

Carnegie Library

Sideways heads
in a room of whispers,
in the domed place

beneath shade trees
on West Main,
our peewee discoveries

were funny rhymes
and horse-back journeys,
myths, space, bugs—

*Don't forget to renew your books,
it's two-cents a day fine,
that's two root beer barrels!—*

and always green Billy,
seed-flinger, his Ben Franklin
cage atop the catalog cards,

our love expressed
with giggles, dirty fingers,
so he might sing sharp notes.

I visited grown-up books
to write a report on him and his kind:
Melopsittacus undulatus,

budgerigars native to Australia,
with color variations, able to mimic
voice and thus their charm.

Is wisdom an adventure,
one insight and another, connecting,
unfolding in your small corner of the stars?

Our corner had a room, guarded
by a green servant of wisdom
for his fourteen years.

Miss Audie's Scotland Slides

Sheep and more sheep, sheep beside the fencerows,
sheep atop a tall hill as we made our way up A77,
and I hoped my pictures of the craggy coast,
its sharp rocks and waves and overcast sky,
turned out well as Henry dared not look,
unused to the British car.

All the small places: Cainryan, Ballantrae, Lendalfoot,
Girvan, Kirkoswald, Maybole. The inns and shops,
always the roundabouts, folks on bicycles,
more sheep on hillsides and cattle,
configurations of green, black and white.

A ship's manifest from Stranraer
has the name of a widow, Rachel McKay
née McGerchie, her daughter Isla and son James,
all who sleep in my home place,
in the family graveyard at Zion's Church.

We settled for the night, and the next day
tried haggis, shopped, walked the high castle,
and I wished I could talk down
the unintelligible clerk on the price of a kilt.
But I still thought of their voyage to Illinois
from the Firth of Clyde, their memories
of craggy shores and storm clouds, now buried
in dust until I, a modest scion,
could say, *Look down from Heaven,*
Mothers and Fathers,
I've come back.

Last Meeting of the Williams Pond Goose Hunting Club

Ten acres
overflowed from Little River

beyond the railroad bridge that fell
with the spring rains of '97

and its fragments of legend:
who killed whom, Jeremiah or Thomas,

who concealed the body in the lake?
Who was hanged?

Men with guns pass time with stories,
in their lodge and in the brush.

Our man boasted of his yearly take,
good eating enough for winter,

"the Canada Geese capital
of the state," where farmers plowed,

turned soil, so the birds came
this far south and talked in their own,

cross way where the buried grain
could be picked at, gathered,

the lake for habitat, majestic
territories. But now, there is no-plow

farming, golf courses
of upstate suburbs offer places of seed

and grain. Geese stay further north,
where men with golf clubs

talk. With parting shots into the air,
the group adjourns from their lodge,

sine die. Toward his car, our man
swears a gander bit him on the ass.

Summer

Shale, conglomerate, sandstone, jasper—
he loved his pyrite,
quarter-sized bit of gold
only a fool would use for money—

basalt, obsidian, granite, gypsum,
rose quartz,
a bit of copper ore from out West,
and petrified wood.
A beginner's set for geology.

He adds ambitions and pastimes,
a kid in summer,

like botany. Wild flowers
by the pond out back: elecampane,
wood sorrel, white clover, ironweed,
spotted touch-me-not....

sleuthing for butterflies:
spring azure, question mark,
zebra swallowtail,
the great spangled fritillary he followed
for yards through the brush.

Rainy days philately: his stamp album,
the Famous American series,
half-cent Ben Franklin
in the Liberty set,
a Clara Barton,
the Immortal Chaplains...

Today, he pilots model planes:
Sopwith Camel, SPAD S.VII,
Niuport 21, Fokker DR,
on the field of his play table

in dogfights with butterflies,

rough landings
in the shale and the clover.

Lucy's Salon

I helped my mother
navigate our small town's sidewalks,
especially where the tree roots pried up
the concrete and she could stumble.

Holding her arm, I opened the door.
Into my face, the blast of AC, smell
of permanents. Inside, Lucy hugged her
and told her she looked pretty.

Mom knew the drill, expected it:
her natural seat, the green apron,
the slow leaning backward
into the sink. *Warm enough, sweetie?*

Mary's looking for choir volunteers.
Herb is finally retiring.
Did you hear Lydia's
transmission went out,

but she can't afford to get it fixed
and doesn't know what to do?
Annie's cancer hasn't come back.
Madge looked up from her *Redbook*.

At the proper time Lucy stood
at the ready to cool hot spots
on Mom's scalp. Then brushing,
another appointment, a goodbye hug.

Helping her back to the car,
I praised Mom's
headful of tight blue curls,
and she beamed with happiness.

1962

The silver, plastic Colt
slips into its holster for the stick-horse ride
from the kitchen and the morning TV news,
into the open range of the backyard.

African violets upon the window sill
the sunny day outside,
dry green beyond Dad's garden.

*What if a fire started and the firemen
couldn't put it out? The world
would burn up.* That was the only way
he knew to ask. *The firemen are good
at what they do*, Mom said.

He practiced lying in the grass
with his hands over his head,
as he learned in first grade. He hoped
he would at least be home from school.
He hoped the foreign leaders would think first
of the children.

Cemetery Caretaker

I mow, and right around
the line of veterans' stones
and their flags, a wheel collapses
into an empty place in the soil:
a vole's tunnel.
I nearly stumble, and kill the engine.

Before too many days
there is a serpentine trace in the grass,
like pictures of hookworms
on the walls of the doctor
where I take my dogs.

*We can trap it
and release it elsewhere,*
says the man at a humane pest service,
but *that's no guarantee it won't return,*
and that's that. Another day,
I surprise wee beast, so we're even.
It scurries from a hole
toward flowers, tiny flags.

The dark earth is what it knows,
but soldiers go violent to the grass
for the sake of folk like me,
to live and work, and tend
the silent places.

Garage Science

If she rides her bike,
her birthday chemistry lab,

the beakers and test tubes
and flasks and substances

will stay safe, for her mom
is laundry busy, and her dad

is in profane prayer
with his tools and pickup motor.

She pours cola from a test tube
onto a soil sample from a vacation trip

to determine the presence
of Bombastium, and

the right mix of sodium carbonate
and sandbox sand could increase

the BTUs of many fossil fuels.
The use of litmus paper

to determine acids and bases
could lead with unforced mastery

to a cancer cure. But now, it's copper,
and two pennies buy an Astro Pop.

Breathing traces of argon, methane, and CO_2
but mostly nitrogen and oxygen,

she pants her bike past Rachel Park
toward little Birch Street market,

where Mrs. Hennessee kindly asks her
how she'll change the world.

Bagworms in the Hands of an Angry Homeowner

A dread of spring,
like sin waiting

for pleasant days:
their nasty shelters

on our evergreens,
blue spruce.

You must spray them
in June, for

they spread quickly,
those horrid sacks

spread like cancer
so your pretty plants

are ruined
by August.

Dreadfully
provoked,

we purchase
a good spray,

or set aside time
to pick them off

and send them,
worthy of nothing else,

to our backyard pit
of hell.

Friends on the Nickel Plate Tracks

How far do you want to go?
How far can you balance on the rails?

We never made it far without falling,
back to crunching in the cinders,

hopping from tie to tie with an eye out
for dated nails, an open ear

for the train, its tremor and breath.
Once we put two pennies on the tracks

and resolved to find them flat
the next time we came this way.

We walked all the way to Hodstown,
to Sam Morton's hundred acres

in sight of Route 38 and Sunday drivers.
What are those kids doing?

Just lazy walkers in summertime,
talking about mean Mrs. Runyon

and her boring class, the way
Donna Burke's eyes sparkled,

and whether we'd remember this
in twenty, thirty years.

Summer Band

Mosquitos and heat
and music in the park,
our bandstand we wanted to forget
then felt sad when it came down last year.

How was band today?
asked Mom. *Everyone hates Mike
because his clarinet squeaks,
and Sarah quit because*

*she has a crush on a singer
in the folk trio. They hold
hootenannies at the park
the same time we practice.*

*My last reed cracked.
Kevin slipped on trombone spit,
Tina sassed Mr. Corwall
and he moved her to third chair.*

What else? she asked.
*I need to sell tickets
to the spaghetti supper
so we can raise money*

for uniforms. We almost have
The Liberty Bell March
and the U.S. Steel Hour Theme
but Along Comes Mary

*is too fast for the cornet section,
and* The Age of Aquarius
*won't dawn this summer.
Mr. Corwall gets a lot of headaches.*

Dair-E-Hut

The afternoon sidewalk
is too hot upon bare feet

as three lines of locals
advance at the same rate.

for vanilla or chocolate,
butter magic, banana swirl.

What do you want? yells a woman
to someone waiting behind.

Sherbets: lime and lemon,
Grape drinks, orange and cherry...

He shifts his feet like a dancer
practicing steps, stands tiptoe.

No, you can't have two,
a dad tells a little kid.

But of course, Grandpa
winks.

At last at the window,
at last in the shade,

A float, or chocolate...
or strawberry,

or butter pecan...
No, it's chocolate.

Barefoot tomorrow,
who knows?

Robot King of Mars

I squared my shoulders and boomed,
I'm the Robot King of Mars,

and Bobby said, *Oh, no,
we're doomed!* and we ran around,

his index finger and thumb sending out
laser beams, till I remembered

I had a right hand, too, and I fired,
too late... Now what?

I could die on the spot, or be knocked
into the abyss

that was the stream, screaming toward
the earth's core, then hide beside the bank

till I emerged as Mud Man,
whose 5th dimension powers

transported his foes
to distant worlds like Mars, with its king.

But Bobby already
flew around the park, speeding

through the trees, showing off
his powers in this yellow sun.

Indermark Crossing

is a place mapped
in community talk, like the crossroads
Foursquare, Polecat Mound near Marytown,

and this spot where Co. 1445 crosses
the Nickel Plate tracks, where you go
to the Bottoms in sight of I-57.

If you look both ways twice, you're fine,
but there's just an old sawbucks sign
with no warning light, and someone could forget,

like the man who awoke to the Lord
while his car lay hundreds of feet down,
parts strewn along the tracks.

Small town folks come to see a mangled car
against the junk yard fence, for respect,
for something to do on an evening,

My god, he would never have known
what happened? How is his family?
his wife and children? Have you heard?

Parents took their teens: *Dear lord,*
look both ways, look again, then look again,
just get your ass across, dear god

as my dad said, twenty-five years later,
so that I can describe the car as if I'd seen it myself,
its crumpled mass, the still blue, wadded doors.

Family Trip

The night time is so black on Route 66
at Meteor Crater after open hours.

Mom's diary: "Albuquerque,
Correo, we passed the Paraje Trading Post,
bathroom break finally at Budville.
Still early morning…"

In the back seat, I read: *the Great Unconformity:*
Cambrian Tapeats sandstone, atop
the metamorphic Vishnu Schist.
500 million years atop 1.7 billion.

"Grants, Prewitt, Thoreau,
an Indian shop at Gallup,
where I got jewelry while Paul's dad honked the horn."

The Cambrian explosion:
diversification of organisms,
the first skeletons and shells,
years of activity in the tens of millions.

"Arizona: Lupton, Sanders, Chambers.
A quick visit to the Petrified Forest, Paul bought a set of rocks."
Goodwater, Holbrook, Meteor Crater, closed.
Night, ten hours from Tucumcari.
No vacancy at the Flagstaff KOA, big fight.
We spend the night in the parking lot.
In the morning, breakfast, U.S. 180 north."

Vishnu and Hakatai shale, Paleozoic layers,
Kaibab and Toroweap down to Bright Angel and Tapeats,
seas advancing, moving, washing away
surface rock, releasing icons from the crustal stone.

The rushing Colorado,
a ride through rapids, sun
baking my brain. At last, the sacred seam.

"Paul's dad said, 'I told you,
we *have to* make time
so Paul can say he put his hand
on the missing billion years...' "

Happiness

How wonderful that the phone booth
still stands, without our initials

thank God, on the corner
of the telephone office

(which is now the senior center)
among our small town's memory places…

Whatever happened to that strawberry girl
whom I met at summer tennis lessons,

who puffed her cheeks
for every photo, even her yearbook?

We talked around town
in a half-embrace, a spoof of clingy teens.

Her mother told her she had big bones,
but that was only one of her troubles.

She liked sad songs that made her cry,
she refused to chew

the ice in her sodas, because people
who chew ice have sex problems.

On Sunday afternoons, I made an excuse
to bike-ride and called her from this phone,

fifty cents for three minutes, and we talked
till the operator interrupted.

I remember *Does she ever think of me?* songs
and wonder, though it's fine if she doesn't,

if she is as happy in her life
as I am in mine.

Kryptonite on July 4th

Metallic green paint
from our hobby shop
is applied to a pocket-size stone.

Rinse the brush in kerosene,
and with that begins
the familiar story:

the chain reaction in the planet's core,
destroying life and the beautiful cities
as humanoid Kal-El sails through space,

followed by glowing meteors of different colors,
non-reactive with oxygen and thus intact
once crashed into places like the backyard

to emit gamma radiation that affects
Superman's photovolaic skin cells,
stealing his energy, risking his life.

The stone was handy for chasing playground girls
(likely Phantom Zone fugitives)
and for boys in the grass, scooping up

grasshoppers to catch their spit
and on the best days kidnapping box turtles
for show and tell

before they amble away.
In summer, he put a cherry bomb

beneath his brilliant stone,
lit it, ran, and watched
Kryptonite fly a good ten feet.

No TV for a week.

Haircut at Elmer's

As clippers buzzed,
I saw my face

in the mirror that faced
the mirror behind us

and the back of my head,
and my face, and my head,

and on and on, so that
I dreamed of infinity

in our small town, map spot
within a mass of dots,

in a state, a nation, a continent,
the globe, the rush of planets

around the sun that was a speck
among galaxy billions,

distances of space and time,
from the Triangulum Galaxy

to the window facing
our town's only stop light,

and me in the barbershop
air rich with colognes, my eye

on the penny candy globe
as clippers buzzed, a child in mirrors

for whom the very (trimmed)
hairs on my head were numbered.

Morels

Grandpa found seventy-five morels beneath a tree!
Where, O where was this?

But he never divulged,
for he couldn't remember, though his eyes twinkled.

He said that was so long ago, the 1910s,
and he was young,

open-eyed, hiking the places
with fallen trees, ash, elm, poplar,

and the sandy black soil on which light
shines on chilly days, so the sclerotium

can germinate to the fruiting mycelium.
But ....that doesn't happen when you want, he said,

It's not like going to the apple tree
and selecting a beauty for your meal.

This is more like a miracle, serendipity of help
that you seek and expect but can't predict

and can't return to, as to a room when
you don't know if you'll be back, or a place

in the woods where you had luck one year
but not the next. In the meantime, be thankful

as you take the nutty treasures home,
soak them free of dirt and ants, cut them

lengthwise, fried them up in butter, and savor
God's earthy gladness, the flavor of place.

Country Pastor

There are days when I look out the window
and try to perceive the timber's separate trees,
each layer of yellow leaves in perspective
in this field, and the next, and the next.

There are days when I pray first
for others, rather than myself,
yet my own worry is a day's first thoughts
my sight's clearest layer from morning till evening.

A large tree may contain two million leaves,
each layer perhaps 200,000. The brain
processes 6 quintillion instructions per second.
Which pertain to God? Don't they all?

The squirrels are out, and the rabbits
are seen only in the dark of dawn and dusk.
Acorns land hard, the leaves teach this season:
don't hold tightly to what passes away.

Autumn flows to winter, spring to summer,
and we will seek God in each new season
upon this rock, third from the sun, the faith
of Peter circling the sun two thousand times.

First Advent Sunday

Unlock the back door,
the way for firewood,
leaves, and snowy mud.

Pin oak, maple,
willow blow in
November wind,

the Canada geese
circle the lake, harsh
migrating angels

at last landing
upon autumn
with a gliding splash.

The painter
in the soft rush
has longed to hear them

as she practices
the color of timber,
cold trees a hedge

for the land's lake,
welcoming
Advent. *Comfort,*

O comfort, people
of the land, she says,
I declare this color

Williams Pond,
purple and brown,
more water than paint.

Small-Town December Saturday

A cold morning's
announced event,

chilly, gray day.
Bundled kids crunch

sugar canes. A few
whine. Parents scold:

Be good for him,
and it is so.

Townsfolk nestle
on the bleachers,

on their blankets,
at the football field

till laughter, cheers
at the Cessna's buzz

and soon the red spot
emerges, down, down,

fatter and fatter,
here he comes, here he comes.

St. Nick from above
lands with his black boots

on the thirty-yard line
(pretty close, not a sleigh

aiming for a rooftop,
after all) and the children

giggle in the field to greet him
as he bounds to the set-up

gingerbread house, promises
for wish after wish,

lifetimes of joy. Elves
wrap the spruce-green chute.

Paved with Stars

I read that an asteroid the size of a bus
slammed into northwestern China,

and another asteroid as large
as our hometown (though

they didn't report it that way:
they said eight square miles)

passed the earth but not close
to harm. Still, say it had hit

our village, that would have ended us
and, likely life on earth, for

the KT extinction is said
to have happened from an asteroid

nine miles wide, struck
at the present Chicxulub

and sent debris into the air, set forests
ablaze: the only warmth in a world

of dark and cold, 10+ Richter quakes,
the end of the dinosaurs, land and ocean

ecosystems, which, as scientists say,
set the stage for mammals including,

eventually, us and all the animals,
and our plants, lakes, rivers and seas

showered night and day with 100 tons
space material that we crunch unaware

beneath our feet and comb from our hair,
and upon all the places we love, for now

safe from whatever befalls us,
our journeys paved with stars.

Psalm in Snow

Deep snowfall, ten degrees.
Our pastor isn't sure
whether to cancel church or not.

We're not sure, either,
no one is, but our neighbor lady
lives for the House of the Lord.

Snow stacks upon the fields of those
who have walked through valleys of shadows,
and Pastor shepherds them.

She perfects her sermon
on goodness and mercy, watches, prays,
makes a snowman with the youth.

Afternoon turns to evening,
the early moonlight is a voice
that is not heard but heard everywhere,

like the calm of the stars,
the timber of the county, hills
and ravines arrayed more than Solomon.

God asks, *have you visited*
the storehouses of snow,
can you loosen the cords of Orion?

We make angels in white, loved by the one
from whom comes the hoar-frost of heaven,
channels of snow, Christ in cold.

Folks and Pastor phone: *let's try to meet.*
You know Miss Audie will come anyway,
and what is snow but still waters?

Paul Stroble teaches philosophy and religious studies at Webster University in St. Louis and is also adjunct faculty at Eden Theological Seminary. Previously he taught at the University of Akron, Indiana University Southeast, Louisville Seminary, and Northern Arizona University. He is a native of Vandalia (Fayette County), Illinois. A grantee of the National Endowment for the Humanities and the Louisville Institute, he has written several books, primarily church related, and numerous articles, essays, and curricular materials. He blogs at paulstroble.blogspot.com. His previous chapbooks with Finishing Line Press, which share the same fictional geography with this one, are *Dreaming at the Electric Hobo* (2015) and *Little River* (2017).

www.ingramcontent.com/pod-product-compliance
Lightning Source LLC
LaVergne TN
LVHW041603070426
835507LV00011B/1287

"*The Relationship Chronicles Straight Talk, Real Love, No Drama!* is a heartfelt, straight-talk read that encourages the reader to assess their mindset, behavior and reactions in their relationships. Judi's transparency gives the reader comfort and courage to conduct a true self-analysis and begin the road to healing, happiness and growth.

—*Kim Sheffield*
Founder and Publisher of Esteem Magazine

In *The Relationship Chronicles Straight Talk, Real Love, No Drama!*, Judi Mason reveals practical ways to avoid pitfalls in relationships. The powerful guidance provided creates ways to build, rebuild, repair and restore relationships to a place of validity and authenticity. This is a must read for men and women seeking successful relationships.

—*David Twyman*
Life Coach & Speaker

One of my favorite sayings is "Self esteem and maturity is the key to a successful relationship." Judi Mason expresses those sentiments in *The Relationship Chronicles Straight Talk, Real Love, No Drama!* This book provides a positive approach to discovering one's self worth and applying that revelation to their relationships.

—*Gwendolyn Tennard Owens*
MA Educator and Mentor